50 Breakfast Bowl Ideas

By: Kelly Johnson

Table of Contents

- Acai Berry Bowl
- Avocado Toast Breakfast Bowl
- Mango Coconut Chia Pudding Bowl
- Peanut Butter Banana Oatmeal Bowl
- Greek Yogurt and Granola Bowl
- Cinnamon Apple Quinoa Bowl
- Sweet Potato and Egg Breakfast Bowl
- Strawberry Almond Smoothie Bowl
- Blueberry Coconut Overnight Oats Bowl
- Chocolate Banana Protein Bowl
- Tropical Fruit Salad Bowl
- Apple Cinnamon Chia Bowl
- Raspberry Almond Butter Bowl
- Spinach and Avocado Quinoa Bowl
- Mixed Berry and Yogurt Bowl
- Mango Chia Pudding Bowl
- Banana Nut Oatmeal Bowl
- Kiwi and Coconut Smoothie Bowl
- Oatmeal with Cinnamon Pears Bowl
- Coconut Yogurt Parfait Bowl
- Smashed Avocado and Egg Bowl
- Cinnamon Toast Crunch Oatmeal Bowl
- Sweet Potato and Kale Breakfast Bowl
- Chocolate Peanut Butter Smoothie Bowl
- Almond Joy Oatmeal Bowl
- Peach and Ricotta Breakfast Bowl
- Lemon Poppy Seed Overnight Oats Bowl
- Strawberry Coconut Quinoa Bowl
- Blueberry Almond Butter Bowl
- Pineapple Coconut Pudding Bowl
- Chia Pudding with Berries and Almonds Bowl
- Roasted Veggie and Quinoa Bowl
- Apple Walnut Oatmeal Bowl
- Mango Banana Smoothie Bowl
- Chocolate Cherry Protein Bowl

- Coconut Milk Rice Pudding Bowl
- Pomegranate and Almond Breakfast Bowl
- Grilled Peach and Yogurt Bowl
- Chia Seed Pudding with Almonds Bowl
- Maple Cinnamon Granola Bowl
- Avocado Mango Smoothie Bowl
- Warm Quinoa Breakfast Bowl with Berries
- Cacao and Banana Oatmeal Bowl
- Almond Butter and Banana Bowl
- Mixed Nut and Fruit Granola Bowl
- Strawberry Chia Jam Bowl
- Green Smoothie Bowl with Spinach and Kale
- Apple Cranberry Quinoa Bowl
- Protein-Packed Berry Oatmeal Bowl
- Kiwi and Coconut Yogurt Bowl

Acai Berry Bowl

Ingredients:

- 1 packet frozen acai berry puree
- 1/2 banana
- 1/2 cup mixed berries (blueberries, strawberries, raspberries)
- 1/4 cup granola
- 1 tbsp chia seeds
- 1/4 cup almond milk (or any milk of choice)
- Honey or agave syrup (optional)

Instructions:

1. In a blender, combine the acai berry puree, banana, mixed berries, and almond milk. Blend until smooth.
2. Pour the acai mixture into a bowl.
3. Top with granola, chia seeds, and extra fresh fruit. Drizzle with honey or syrup if desired. Serve immediately.

Avocado Toast Breakfast Bowl

Ingredients:

- 1 ripe avocado, mashed
- 2 eggs, scrambled or fried
- 1/2 cup cherry tomatoes, halved
- 1/4 cup red onion, thinly sliced
- 1 tbsp olive oil
- Salt and pepper, to taste
- 1/2 tsp red pepper flakes (optional)
- 1-2 slices whole-grain toast, crumbled

Instructions:

1. In a bowl, mash the avocado and season with salt, pepper, and red pepper flakes.
2. In a pan, scramble or fry the eggs to your liking.
3. To assemble the bowl, layer the mashed avocado, scrambled eggs, cherry tomatoes, red onion, and crumbled toast.
4. Drizzle with olive oil and top with extra seasonings, if desired. Serve immediately.

Mango Coconut Chia Pudding Bowl

Ingredients:

- 1/4 cup chia seeds
- 1 cup coconut milk
- 1/2 ripe mango, diced
- 1 tbsp shredded coconut
- 1 tbsp honey or maple syrup

Instructions:

1. In a bowl, mix the chia seeds, coconut milk, and honey/maple syrup. Stir to combine.
2. Cover and refrigerate for at least 4 hours or overnight to let the chia seeds absorb the liquid and thicken.
3. Top with fresh mango and shredded coconut before serving. Enjoy chilled.

Peanut Butter Banana Oatmeal Bowl

Ingredients:

- 1/2 cup rolled oats
- 1 cup milk (or any milk alternative)
- 1/2 banana, sliced
- 1 tbsp peanut butter
- 1 tbsp chia seeds (optional)
- 1 tsp honey or maple syrup (optional)

Instructions:

1. Cook the oats according to package instructions, using the milk to cook them.
2. Once the oatmeal is ready, stir in the peanut butter until smooth.
3. Top with sliced banana, chia seeds, and a drizzle of honey or maple syrup. Serve warm.

Greek Yogurt and Granola Bowl

Ingredients:

- 1 cup Greek yogurt
- 1/2 cup granola
- 1/4 cup mixed berries (strawberries, blueberries, etc.)
- 1 tbsp honey or agave syrup
- 1 tbsp almonds or walnuts, chopped (optional)

Instructions:

1. In a bowl, spoon in the Greek yogurt.
2. Top with granola, mixed berries, and chopped nuts if using.
3. Drizzle with honey or agave syrup for added sweetness. Serve immediately.

Cinnamon Apple Quinoa Bowl

Ingredients:

- 1/2 cup cooked quinoa
- 1 apple, diced
- 1/2 tsp ground cinnamon
- 1 tbsp honey or maple syrup
- 1 tbsp walnuts or almonds, chopped (optional)
- 1/4 cup milk (optional)

Instructions:

1. In a small pan, sauté the diced apple with cinnamon until soft, about 3-4 minutes.
2. In a bowl, combine the cooked quinoa with the sautéed apples.
3. Drizzle with honey or maple syrup and top with chopped nuts. Add a splash of milk for extra creaminess if desired. Serve warm.

Sweet Potato and Egg Breakfast Bowl

Ingredients:

- 1 small sweet potato, peeled and diced
- 2 eggs (scrambled, fried, or poached)
- 1/4 avocado, sliced
- 1/4 cup black beans (optional)
- 1 tbsp olive oil
- Salt and pepper, to taste

Instructions:

1. Heat olive oil in a pan and cook the diced sweet potato until tender, about 10 minutes. Season with salt and pepper.
2. While the sweet potatoes are cooking, scramble, fry, or poach the eggs.
3. To assemble the bowl, layer the sweet potatoes, eggs, avocado slices, and black beans (if using). Serve warm.

Strawberry Almond Smoothie Bowl

Ingredients:

- 1 cup frozen strawberries
- 1/2 banana
- 1/2 cup almond milk (or milk of choice)
- 1 tbsp almond butter
- 1 tbsp sliced almonds
- 1 tbsp chia seeds

Instructions:

1. In a blender, combine frozen strawberries, banana, almond milk, and almond butter. Blend until smooth.
2. Pour the smoothie into a bowl and top with sliced almonds and chia seeds. Serve immediately.

Blueberry Coconut Overnight Oats Bowl

Ingredients:

- 1/2 cup rolled oats
- 1/2 cup coconut milk (or any milk of choice)
- 1/4 cup fresh or frozen blueberries
- 1 tbsp shredded coconut
- 1 tbsp honey or maple syrup (optional)
- 1 tbsp chia seeds (optional)

Instructions:

1. In a bowl, combine the oats, coconut milk, blueberries, shredded coconut, honey, and chia seeds.
2. Stir well, cover, and refrigerate overnight.
3. In the morning, give it a stir and enjoy your creamy blueberry coconut overnight oats!

Chocolate Banana Protein Bowl

Ingredients:

- 1 ripe banana, sliced
- 1/2 cup chocolate protein powder
- 1/2 cup almond milk (or any milk of choice)
- 1 tbsp almond butter or peanut butter
- 1 tbsp cacao nibs (optional)
- 1 tbsp chia seeds (optional)

Instructions:

1. In a blender, combine the banana, protein powder, almond milk, and almond butter. Blend until smooth.
2. Pour into a bowl and top with cacao nibs and chia seeds for extra texture and nutrients.
3. Enjoy your protein-packed, chocolatey breakfast!

Tropical Fruit Salad Bowl

Ingredients:

- 1/2 cup diced pineapple
- 1/2 cup diced mango
- 1/2 cup diced papaya
- 1/2 banana, sliced
- 1 tbsp shredded coconut
- 1 tbsp lime juice

Instructions:

1. Combine the diced pineapple, mango, papaya, and banana in a bowl.
2. Drizzle with lime juice and toss gently.
3. Top with shredded coconut and serve immediately for a refreshing tropical fruit salad.

Apple Cinnamon Chia Bowl

Ingredients:

- 1/2 cup rolled oats
- 1/2 cup milk of choice
- 1/4 cup apple, diced
- 1/2 tsp ground cinnamon
- 1 tbsp chia seeds
- 1 tbsp maple syrup or honey (optional)

Instructions:

1. In a bowl, combine the oats, milk, diced apple, cinnamon, and chia seeds. Stir to combine.
2. Cover and refrigerate overnight.
3. In the morning, stir and add maple syrup or honey for sweetness. Enjoy your warm, spiced apple chia bowl!

Raspberry Almond Butter Bowl

Ingredients:

- 1/2 cup fresh raspberries
- 1 tbsp almond butter
- 1/2 banana, sliced
- 1 tbsp chia seeds
- 1/4 cup granola (optional)

Instructions:

1. In a bowl, layer the raspberries, almond butter, and sliced banana.
2. Sprinkle with chia seeds and granola if desired.
3. Serve immediately and enjoy the creamy almond butter with the tart raspberries.

Spinach and Avocado Quinoa Bowl

Ingredients:

- 1/2 cup cooked quinoa
- 1/2 cup fresh spinach
- 1/4 avocado, sliced
- 1 boiled egg, sliced (optional)
- Salt and pepper to taste
- 1 tbsp olive oil or lemon juice (optional)

Instructions:

1. In a bowl, layer the cooked quinoa, spinach, and avocado slices.
2. If using, add a boiled egg on top for extra protein.
3. Drizzle with olive oil or lemon juice and season with salt and pepper. Serve immediately.

Mixed Berry and Yogurt Bowl

Ingredients:

- 1 cup mixed berries (strawberries, blueberries, raspberries)
- 1 cup Greek yogurt
- 1 tbsp honey or agave syrup
- 1 tbsp granola (optional)

Instructions:

1. In a bowl, layer the Greek yogurt with the mixed berries.
2. Drizzle with honey or syrup and top with granola if desired.
3. Serve immediately for a creamy, berry-packed breakfast.

Mango Chia Pudding Bowl

Ingredients:

- 1/4 cup chia seeds
- 1 cup coconut milk (or any milk of choice)
- 1/2 cup diced mango
- 1 tbsp shredded coconut
- 1 tbsp honey or maple syrup (optional)

Instructions:

1. In a bowl, mix the chia seeds and coconut milk. Stir well and let sit for at least 4 hours or overnight to thicken.
2. Top the chia pudding with fresh diced mango and shredded coconut.
3. Drizzle with honey or maple syrup if desired. Enjoy your tropical chia pudding bowl!

Banana Nut Oatmeal Bowl

Ingredients:

- 1/2 cup rolled oats
- 1 cup milk of choice
- 1 ripe banana, sliced
- 1 tbsp chopped walnuts
- 1 tsp cinnamon
- 1 tbsp honey or maple syrup (optional)

Instructions:

1. In a pot, combine the oats and milk. Cook over medium heat, stirring occasionally, until the oats are soft and creamy (about 5-7 minutes).
2. Pour the oatmeal into a bowl and top with banana slices, chopped walnuts, and cinnamon.
3. Drizzle with honey or maple syrup if desired. Serve warm and enjoy!

Kiwi and Coconut Smoothie Bowl

Ingredients:

- 1 ripe kiwi, peeled and chopped
- 1/2 cup coconut milk (or any milk of choice)
- 1/4 cup frozen mango chunks
- 1 tbsp shredded coconut
- 1 tbsp honey or agave syrup (optional)
- Fresh kiwi slices for garnish

Instructions:

1. In a blender, combine the chopped kiwi, coconut milk, frozen mango, and honey. Blend until smooth.
2. Pour the smoothie into a bowl and top with shredded coconut and fresh kiwi slices.
3. Enjoy the refreshing tropical flavors!

Oatmeal with Cinnamon Pears Bowl

Ingredients:

- 1/2 cup rolled oats
- 1 cup milk of choice
- 1 pear, diced
- 1/2 tsp cinnamon
- 1 tbsp maple syrup (optional)

Instructions:

1. In a saucepan, cook the oats with the milk over medium heat until soft and creamy.
2. In a separate pan, sauté the diced pear with cinnamon for 2-3 minutes until tender.
3. Top the cooked oatmeal with the sautéed pears and drizzle with maple syrup if desired. Serve warm and enjoy!

Coconut Yogurt Parfait Bowl

Ingredients:

- 1 cup coconut yogurt (or any yogurt of choice)
- 1/2 cup granola
- 1/2 cup mixed berries
- 1 tbsp shredded coconut
- 1 tbsp honey or agave syrup (optional)
Instructions:
1. In a bowl, layer the coconut yogurt, granola, and mixed berries.
2. Sprinkle shredded coconut on top and drizzle with honey or agave syrup if desired.
3. Serve immediately for a creamy, crunchy parfait!

Smashed Avocado and Egg Bowl

Ingredients:

- 1 ripe avocado, mashed
- 1 egg, cooked to your liking (boiled, scrambled, or fried)
- Salt and pepper to taste
- 1 tbsp olive oil (optional)

Instructions:

1. Mash the ripe avocado in a bowl and season with salt and pepper.
2. Cook the egg as desired and place it on top of the mashed avocado.
3. Drizzle with olive oil if desired and serve immediately for a filling and nutritious breakfast bowl.

Cinnamon Toast Crunch Oatmeal Bowl

Ingredients:

- 1/2 cup rolled oats
- 1 cup milk of choice
- 1 tbsp ground cinnamon
- 1 tbsp brown sugar
- 1/4 cup crushed Cinnamon Toast Crunch cereal

Instructions:

1. In a pot, cook the oats with the milk over medium heat until creamy.
2. Stir in the ground cinnamon and brown sugar.
3. Pour the oatmeal into a bowl and top with crushed Cinnamon Toast Crunch cereal for a crunchy, cinnamon-sweet finish!

Sweet Potato and Kale Breakfast Bowl

Ingredients:

- 1 medium sweet potato, peeled and diced
- 1/2 cup kale, chopped
- 1 tbsp olive oil
- 1 egg, cooked to your liking
- Salt and pepper to taste

Instructions:

1. Roast the diced sweet potato in olive oil at 400°F (200°C) for 20-25 minutes until tender.
2. Sauté the chopped kale in a pan until wilted (about 2-3 minutes).
3. In a bowl, layer the roasted sweet potato, sautéed kale, and your egg of choice. Season with salt and pepper, then serve immediately.

Chocolate Peanut Butter Smoothie Bowl

Ingredients:

- 1 banana, frozen
- 2 tbsp peanut butter
- 1 tbsp cocoa powder
- 1/2 cup almond milk (or any milk of choice)
- 1 tbsp chocolate chips (optional)

Instructions:

1. In a blender, combine the frozen banana, peanut butter, cocoa powder, and almond milk. Blend until smooth and thick.
2. Pour into a bowl and top with chocolate chips for extra sweetness.
3. Enjoy this decadent smoothie bowl with a hint of chocolate and peanut butter!

Almond Joy Oatmeal Bowl

Ingredients:

- 1/2 cup rolled oats
- 1 cup almond milk (or milk of choice)
- 1 tbsp almond butter
- 1 tbsp unsweetened shredded coconut
- 2 tbsp chopped almonds
- 1 tbsp cacao nibs (optional)
- 1/2 tbsp honey or maple syrup
- 1/4 cup dark chocolate chips (optional)

Instructions:

1. Cook the rolled oats in almond milk over medium heat until creamy and thickened, about 5 minutes.
2. Once the oatmeal is ready, stir in almond butter, shredded coconut, chopped almonds, and cacao nibs (if using).
3. Drizzle with honey or maple syrup and top with dark chocolate chips for a sweet finish.
4. Enjoy a delicious bowl reminiscent of the famous Almond Joy candy bar, packed with healthy fats and antioxidants!

Peach and Ricotta Breakfast Bowl

Ingredients:

- 1/2 cup ricotta cheese
- 1 peach, sliced
- 1 tbsp honey
- 1/4 tsp cinnamon
- 1/4 cup granola (for topping)
- Fresh mint for garnish (optional)

Instructions:

1. In a bowl, place the ricotta cheese as the base.
2. Arrange the sliced peach on top of the ricotta.
3. Drizzle with honey and sprinkle with cinnamon for added sweetness and warmth.
4. Top with granola for crunch and garnish with fresh mint if desired.
5. Enjoy this creamy, fruity, and satisfying breakfast bowl!

Lemon Poppy Seed Overnight Oats Bowl

Ingredients:

- 1/2 cup rolled oats
- 1/2 cup almond milk (or milk of choice)
- 1/2 tsp lemon zest
- 1 tbsp lemon juice
- 1 tsp poppy seeds
- 1 tbsp honey or maple syrup
- Fresh berries or fruit for topping

Instructions:

1. In a jar or bowl, combine the rolled oats, almond milk, lemon zest, lemon juice, and poppy seeds.
2. Stir well, cover, and refrigerate overnight.
3. In the morning, give the oats a good stir and top with fresh berries or fruit of your choice.
4. Enjoy this tangy, refreshing, and healthy breakfast that's packed with fiber and antioxidants!

Strawberry Coconut Quinoa Bowl

Ingredients:

- 1/2 cup cooked quinoa
- 1/2 cup fresh strawberries, sliced
- 1 tbsp shredded coconut
- 1 tbsp honey or maple syrup
- 1/2 tsp vanilla extract
- 1/4 cup almond milk

Instructions:

1. In a small saucepan, heat the cooked quinoa with almond milk and vanilla extract until warm.
2. Spoon the quinoa into a bowl and top with fresh strawberries, shredded coconut, and a drizzle of honey or maple syrup.
3. This sweet and tropical quinoa bowl is rich in protein and perfect for a satisfying breakfast!

Blueberry Almond Butter Bowl

Ingredients:

- 1/2 cup Greek yogurt or dairy-free yogurt
- 1/2 cup blueberries
- 1 tbsp almond butter
- 1 tbsp honey or maple syrup
- 1 tbsp sliced almonds
- 1 tbsp chia seeds (optional)

Instructions:

1. Spoon the Greek yogurt into a bowl as your base.
2. Top with fresh blueberries, a dollop of almond butter, and a drizzle of honey or maple syrup.
3. Sprinkle with sliced almonds and chia seeds for added texture and nutrition.
4. This protein-packed bowl is perfect for a quick, nourishing breakfast!

Pineapple Coconut Pudding Bowl

Ingredients:

- 1/2 cup coconut milk (or milk of choice)
- 1 tbsp chia seeds
- 1/4 tsp vanilla extract
- 1/4 cup fresh pineapple, chopped
- 1 tbsp shredded coconut
- 1 tbsp honey or maple syrup

Instructions:

1. In a jar or bowl, combine the coconut milk, chia seeds, and vanilla extract. Stir well and let it sit for at least 4 hours or overnight in the fridge to thicken.
2. In the morning, top with fresh pineapple, shredded coconut, and a drizzle of honey or maple syrup.
3. Enjoy a tropical, creamy breakfast that's high in fiber and healthy fats!

Chia Pudding with Berries and Almonds Bowl

Ingredients:

- 1/2 cup almond milk (or milk of choice)
- 2 tbsp chia seeds
- 1 tsp vanilla extract
- 1 tbsp honey or maple syrup
- 1/4 cup mixed berries (blueberries, raspberries, etc.)
- 1 tbsp sliced almonds

Instructions:

1. Combine almond milk, chia seeds, and vanilla extract in a jar or bowl. Stir well and refrigerate overnight to let the chia seeds expand and form a pudding-like consistency.
2. In the morning, give the pudding a good stir and top with mixed berries and sliced almonds.
3. This delicious and nutritious chia pudding bowl is packed with fiber, antioxidants, and healthy fats!

Roasted Veggie and Quinoa Bowl

Ingredients:

- 1/2 cup cooked quinoa
- 1/2 cup roasted vegetables (such as sweet potatoes, bell peppers, and zucchini)
- 1/4 cup hummus or tahini
- 1 tbsp pumpkin seeds
- Fresh herbs for garnish (optional)

Instructions:

1. In a bowl, place the cooked quinoa as the base.
2. Add the roasted vegetables on top of the quinoa.
3. Drizzle with hummus or tahini and sprinkle with pumpkin seeds.
4. Garnish with fresh herbs if desired.
5. This savory, nutrient-dense breakfast bowl is packed with fiber, healthy fats, and plant-based protein to start your day right!

Apple Walnut Oatmeal Bowl

Ingredients:

- 1/2 cup rolled oats
- 1 cup almond milk (or milk of choice)
- 1 apple, diced
- 1/4 cup chopped walnuts
- 1/2 tsp cinnamon
- 1 tbsp honey or maple syrup
- Pinch of salt

Instructions:

1. In a saucepan, combine the rolled oats, almond milk, and a pinch of salt. Cook over medium heat, stirring occasionally, until the oats are tender and creamy (about 5-7 minutes).
2. In the last minute of cooking, stir in the cinnamon and diced apple to warm through.
3. Serve the oatmeal in a bowl, topping with chopped walnuts and a drizzle of honey or maple syrup.
4. Enjoy a comforting, nutritious breakfast full of fiber and healthy fats!

Mango Banana Smoothie Bowl

Ingredients:

- 1/2 ripe mango, peeled and chopped
- 1 ripe banana
- 1/2 cup Greek yogurt (or dairy-free yogurt)
- 1/4 cup almond milk (or milk of choice)
- 1 tbsp chia seeds (optional)
- 1/4 cup granola (for topping)
- Sliced fruit for garnish (such as kiwi or coconut flakes)

Instructions:

1. In a blender, combine the mango, banana, Greek yogurt, and almond milk. Blend until smooth and creamy.
2. Pour the smoothie into a bowl and top with chia seeds (if using), granola, and additional sliced fruit.
3. Enjoy this refreshing, tropical smoothie bowl packed with vitamins and antioxidants!

Chocolate Cherry Protein Bowl

Ingredients:

- 1/2 cup frozen cherries
- 1/2 frozen banana
- 1 scoop chocolate protein powder
- 1/4 cup almond milk (or milk of choice)
- 1 tbsp almond butter
- 1 tbsp cacao nibs (optional)
- 1/4 cup granola for topping

Instructions:

1. In a blender, combine the frozen cherries, banana, chocolate protein powder, almond milk, and almond butter. Blend until smooth and creamy.
2. Pour the smoothie into a bowl and top with cacao nibs and granola for added texture and crunch.
3. Enjoy a protein-packed, deliciously chocolatey breakfast bowl!

Coconut Milk Rice Pudding Bowl

Ingredients:

- 1/2 cup cooked rice (preferably short-grain or arborio)
- 1 cup coconut milk
- 1 tbsp maple syrup
- 1/2 tsp cinnamon
- 1/4 tsp vanilla extract
- 1/4 cup fresh fruit (such as berries or mango)
- Toasted coconut flakes for topping

Instructions:

1. In a saucepan, combine the cooked rice, coconut milk, maple syrup, cinnamon, and vanilla extract. Cook over low heat, stirring occasionally, until the pudding is warm and thickened (about 5-7 minutes).
2. Spoon the rice pudding into a bowl, then top with fresh fruit and toasted coconut flakes.
3. Enjoy a creamy, comforting bowl of coconut rice pudding that's rich and satisfying!

Pomegranate and Almond Breakfast Bowl

Ingredients:

- 1/2 cup Greek yogurt (or dairy-free yogurt)
- 1/4 cup pomegranate seeds
- 1 tbsp almond butter
- 1 tbsp sliced almonds
- 1 tbsp honey or maple syrup
- 1 tbsp chia seeds

Instructions:

1. Spoon the Greek yogurt into a bowl as the base.
2. Top with pomegranate seeds, almond butter, sliced almonds, and chia seeds.
3. Drizzle with honey or maple syrup for sweetness.
4. Enjoy this nutrient-packed bowl that combines the richness of almonds with the refreshing burst of pomegranate!

Grilled Peach and Yogurt Bowl

Ingredients:

- 2 ripe peaches, halved and pitted
- 1/2 cup Greek yogurt (or dairy-free yogurt)
- 1 tbsp honey or maple syrup
- 1 tbsp chia seeds (optional)
- Crumbled granola for topping

Instructions:

1. Preheat the grill or a grill pan over medium heat. Grill the peach halves for about 2-3 minutes on each side, until caramelized and slightly charred.
2. Spoon the Greek yogurt into a bowl. Top with the grilled peach halves, drizzle with honey or maple syrup, and sprinkle with chia seeds and granola.
3. Enjoy the sweet and smoky flavor combination of grilled peaches and creamy yogurt!

Chia Seed Pudding with Almonds Bowl

Ingredients:

- 1/2 cup almond milk (or milk of choice)
- 2 tbsp chia seeds
- 1 tsp vanilla extract
- 1 tbsp maple syrup
- 1/4 cup sliced almonds
- Fresh fruit for topping (such as berries or bananas)

Instructions:

1. In a jar or bowl, combine almond milk, chia seeds, vanilla extract, and maple syrup. Stir well and refrigerate overnight.
2. In the morning, give the pudding a good stir and top with sliced almonds and fresh fruit.
3. Enjoy a healthy and fiber-rich breakfast that's simple to prepare and full of protein!

Maple Cinnamon Granola Bowl

Ingredients:

- 1/2 cup Greek yogurt (or dairy-free yogurt)
- 1/4 cup granola
- 1 tbsp maple syrup
- 1/2 tsp cinnamon
- 1/4 cup fresh fruit (such as berries or bananas)
- 1 tbsp chopped nuts (optional)

Instructions:

1. Spoon the Greek yogurt into a bowl as your base.
2. Top with granola, a drizzle of maple syrup, and a sprinkle of cinnamon.
3. Add fresh fruit and chopped nuts for extra texture and flavor.
4. Enjoy this crunchy, sweet, and nourishing breakfast bowl!

Avocado Mango Smoothie Bowl

Ingredients:

- 1/2 ripe avocado
- 1/2 ripe mango, peeled and chopped
- 1 frozen banana
- 1/2 cup coconut milk (or milk of choice)
- 1/4 cup Greek yogurt (optional)
- Toppings: chia seeds, granola, sliced almonds, fresh fruit (mango, berries)

Instructions:

1. In a blender, combine avocado, mango, banana, coconut milk, and Greek yogurt. Blend until smooth and creamy.
2. Pour the smoothie into a bowl and top with chia seeds, granola, sliced almonds, and fresh fruit.
3. Enjoy this refreshing and creamy smoothie bowl that's perfect for a tropical breakfast!

Warm Quinoa Breakfast Bowl with Berries

Ingredients:

- 1/2 cup cooked quinoa
- 1/2 cup almond milk (or milk of choice)
- 1 tbsp maple syrup or honey
- 1/4 tsp cinnamon
- 1/4 cup mixed berries (strawberries, blueberries, raspberries)
- 1 tbsp chia seeds or flax seeds (optional)

Instructions:

1. In a saucepan, warm the cooked quinoa with almond milk, maple syrup, and cinnamon over low heat for 2-3 minutes, stirring occasionally.
2. Transfer to a bowl and top with fresh mixed berries and chia seeds or flax seeds.
3. Enjoy this protein-packed breakfast that's both warm and comforting!

Cacao and Banana Oatmeal Bowl

Ingredients:

- 1/2 cup rolled oats
- 1 cup almond milk (or milk of choice)
- 1 ripe banana, sliced
- 1 tbsp cacao powder
- 1 tbsp maple syrup or honey
- 1/4 tsp vanilla extract
- Toppings: banana slices, cacao nibs, and walnuts (optional)

Instructions:

1. In a saucepan, bring almond milk to a simmer, then stir in rolled oats. Cook for 5-7 minutes, stirring occasionally.
2. Once the oatmeal is creamy, stir in cacao powder, maple syrup, and vanilla extract.
3. Transfer the oatmeal to a bowl and top with banana slices, cacao nibs, and walnuts for crunch.
4. Enjoy a chocolatey, rich breakfast full of antioxidants and fiber!

Almond Butter and Banana Bowl

Ingredients:

- 1 ripe banana, sliced
- 1 tbsp almond butter
- 1/2 cup Greek yogurt (or dairy-free yogurt)
- 1 tbsp chia seeds
- 1/4 cup granola
- Drizzle of honey or maple syrup

Instructions:

1. Spoon Greek yogurt into a bowl and spread almond butter on top.
2. Add sliced banana, chia seeds, and granola.
3. Drizzle with honey or maple syrup to taste.
4. Enjoy this simple yet filling breakfast bowl packed with protein, healthy fats, and fiber!

Mixed Nut and Fruit Granola Bowl

Ingredients:

- 1/2 cup Greek yogurt (or dairy-free yogurt)
- 1/4 cup granola
- 1/4 cup mixed nuts (almonds, walnuts, pecans)
- 1/4 cup fresh fruit (such as berries, banana, or apple slices)
- 1 tbsp honey or maple syrup (optional)

Instructions:

1. Spoon Greek yogurt into a bowl.
2. Top with granola, mixed nuts, and fresh fruit.
3. Drizzle with honey or maple syrup if desired.
4. Enjoy this crunchy, protein-packed breakfast that's great for a quick, energizing start to your day!

Strawberry Chia Jam Bowl

Ingredients:

- 1 cup fresh strawberries, hulled and chopped
- 2 tbsp chia seeds
- 1-2 tbsp maple syrup or honey
- 1/2 cup Greek yogurt (or dairy-free yogurt)
- 1/4 cup granola
- Fresh strawberries for topping

Instructions:

1. In a bowl, combine the chopped strawberries, chia seeds, and maple syrup. Stir well and let it sit in the refrigerator for at least 30 minutes to allow the chia seeds to thicken and create a jam-like consistency.
2. Spoon Greek yogurt into a bowl and top with the strawberry chia jam.
3. Add granola and fresh strawberry slices on top.
4. Enjoy a sweet and tangy breakfast that's full of fiber and antioxidants!

Green Smoothie Bowl with Spinach and Kale

Ingredients:

- 1/2 cup frozen spinach
- 1/2 cup frozen kale
- 1 frozen banana
- 1/2 cup almond milk (or milk of choice)
- 1 tbsp almond butter
- Toppings: chia seeds, granola, sliced banana, coconut flakes

Instructions:

1. In a blender, combine spinach, kale, frozen banana, almond milk, and almond butter. Blend until smooth and creamy.
2. Pour the smoothie into a bowl.
3. Top with chia seeds, granola, sliced banana, and coconut flakes for added crunch and flavor.
4. Enjoy a nutrient-packed, green smoothie bowl that's perfect for a fresh start to your day!

Apple Cranberry Quinoa Bowl

Ingredients:

- 1/2 cup cooked quinoa
- 1/2 cup unsweetened almond milk (or milk of choice)
- 1/2 apple, diced
- 1/4 cup dried cranberries
- 1/4 tsp cinnamon
- 1 tbsp honey or maple syrup
- Toppings: chopped nuts (walnuts or almonds), fresh apple slices

Instructions:

1. In a saucepan, heat the cooked quinoa with almond milk, cinnamon, and maple syrup over medium heat for 3-4 minutes.
2. Once warm, transfer the quinoa to a bowl and stir in diced apples and dried cranberries.
3. Top with chopped nuts and fresh apple slices for crunch.
4. Enjoy a warm, hearty breakfast that's rich in protein and antioxidants!

Protein-Packed Berry Oatmeal Bowl

Ingredients:

- 1/2 cup rolled oats
- 1 cup almond milk (or milk of choice)
- 1/2 cup mixed berries (blueberries, strawberries, raspberries)

- 1 tbsp chia seeds
- 1 scoop protein powder (optional)
- 1 tbsp almond butter
- Toppings: sliced almonds, fresh berries

Instructions:

1. In a saucepan, bring almond milk to a simmer and stir in rolled oats. Cook for 5-7 minutes, stirring occasionally.
2. Once the oatmeal is thick and creamy, stir in the protein powder (if using) and almond butter.
3. Pour the oatmeal into a bowl and top with mixed berries, chia seeds, and sliced almonds.
4. Enjoy this protein-packed, fiber-rich breakfast that's both filling and nutritious!

Kiwi and Coconut Yogurt Bowl

Ingredients:

- 1/2 cup coconut yogurt (or regular yogurt)
- 1 kiwi, peeled and sliced
- 1/4 cup granola
- 1 tbsp shredded coconut
- 1 tbsp chia seeds
- Honey or maple syrup (optional)

Instructions:

1. Spoon coconut yogurt into a bowl.
2. Top with sliced kiwi, granola, shredded coconut, and chia seeds.
3. Drizzle with honey or maple syrup for added sweetness if desired.
4. Enjoy this tropical-inspired yogurt bowl that's full of vitamins and healthy fats!

www.ingramcontent.com/pod-product-compliance
Lightning Source LLC
LaVergne TN
LVHW081332060526
838201LV00055B/2590